The Norfolk Coast

THE NORFOLK COAST

Jon Gibbs

FRANCES LINCOLN LIMITED
PUBLISHERS

ABOVE, LEFT TO RIGHT Burnham Overy Staithe, Holkham Bay, Hunstanton, Morston.

To my family for their love and support.

Frances Lincoln Ltd
4 Torriano Mews
Torriano Avenue
London NW5 2RZ
www.franceslincoln.com

First Frances Lincoln edition 2010

A catalogue record for this book is available from the British Library.

ISBN 978-0-7112-2982-2

Printed bound in China

HALF TITLE Great Yarmouth.

TITLE PAGE Happisburgh.

CONTENTS

BLAKENEY

INTRODUCTION

LEFT Blakeney.

The Norfolk Coast is an incredibly varied part of the English coastline. Along its length the various landscapes include dunes, cliffs, saltmarshes, shingle, mudflats and golden sandy beaches. Throw in a smattering of seaside resorts and sleepy harbour villages, nature reserves and a coastal path, and you have an area suitable for many types of visitor, from wildlife watchers to walkers or those who would rather let the day pass them by as they recline in a deckchair.

The coast has always held a fascination for me. Its ever-changing nature, shaped by the actions of the sea or weather, makes every visit unique. Without wanting to go too poetic it is a place where you can 'feel the weather', a meeting point between the elements of the earth, water and air.

Photographing the images for this book has given me the opportunity to visit some new places and to walk on parts of the coastal path I had never trodden before. Many of these new places have become photographic favourites of mine and this makes the decision on where to shoot on my future local photographic trips so much the harder – this coast really does have an embarrassment of riches.

My photographic journey starts from my own part of the world on the East Norfolk Coast at Gorleston-on-Sea, the neighbouring town to my hometown of Great Yarmouth. It continues in an anti-clockwise direction in a kind of semi-circle shape finishing on the west-facing part of the coast, in the case of this book at Snettisham.

Rather than giving a breakdown of the areas in this introduction, I will let the changes in the coastal landscape show themselves in the pictures and give you an insight into the various locations in the text accompanying the pictures.

I hope you enjoy the pictures of this special coastline.

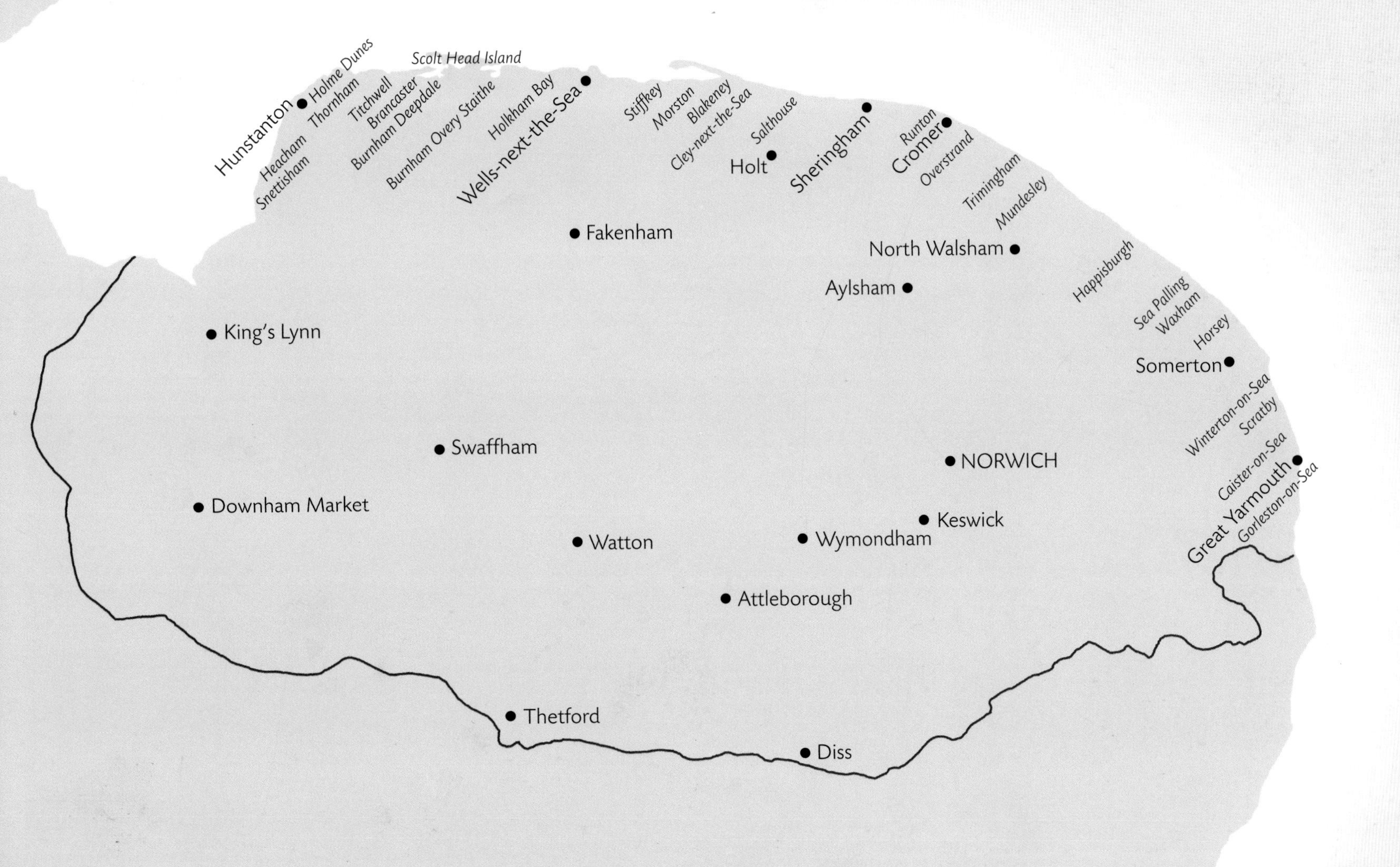

GORLESTON-ON-SEA

Gorleston-on-Sea first developed as a seaside resort at the beginning of the twentieth century, and its seafront has a far more genteel atmosphere than its neighbour Great Yarmouth on the other side of the River Yare.

On the right of the picture is the harbour's entrance, where the River Yare joins the North Sea.

The building to the far left is the Gorleston Pavilion, which was built in 1901, with beautiful Art Nouveau decoration. It still provides a full programme of year-round entertainment.

BELOW A moody morning on the pier at Gorleston-on-Sea, with the coast guard station and an oil rig supply vessel heading out into the North Sea.

Just visible in the distance on the left of the picture is the barge that was used in the initial work on the Great Yarmouth Outer Harbour Project. The project will enable larger ships to visit the port, thereby opening new freight routes between Great Yarmouth and Europe and hopefully bringing much-needed revenue to the local area.

OVERLEAF A distinctive feature of the pier at Gorleston-on-Sea is the breakwater, which is always a great place to watch a stormy North Sea in action.

GREAT YARMOUTH

Great Yarmouth is the largest seaside resort on the Norfolk Coast. The 'Golden Mile' seafront has all the usual attractions one would associate with an English seaside resort.

The town has two piers, the Britannia and the Wellington. This picture shows Britannia Pier on a spring morning. There has been a pier on this site since the 1850s, the present buildings dating from the late 1950s. Previous buildings had been lost to a spate of fires in the early twentieth century. In the distance on the far left of the picture are the two huge cranes of the outer harbour, which will be completed in 2010.

ABOVE A solitary disused boat sits on the North Beach at Great Yarmouth under a dramatic summer evening sky. In the distance out to sea is the Scroby Sands Windfarm.

RIGHT Dramatic conditions on a summer evening, with Scroby Sands Windfarm and an intense electrical storm.

The thirty-turbine windfarm sits 3 miles out in the North Sea and has become a major attraction for visitors to the town.

CAISTER-ON-SEA

RIGHT A half sunken pill box, driftwood and a stormy sea at Caister-on-Sea, a village north of Great Yarmouth.

Caister-on-Sea has had a voluntary lifeboat service since 1973 after the closure of its RNLI Station in 1969.

'Caister men never turn back' is a local phrase that sums up the courage of those lifeboatmen lost in the Caister Lifeboat Disaster of 1901. It is just as befitting a phrase to those who man the lifeboat today, giving their time freely and putting themselves at risk to save others.

FAR RIGHT Stormy conditions on a September morning at Caister-on-Sea.

CALIFORNIA AND SCRATBY

The small villages of California and Scratby sit atop cliffs that start to form north of Caister-on-Sea.

This picture, taken on a moody November day, shows the view northwards from the cliffs. As in many other parts of Norfolk, coastal erosion is rife here. These houses are very safe at the moment but the day will surely come when they will sit on the cliff edge.

Beautiful early light on the beach at California.

WINTERTON-ON-SEA

LEFT BELOW The village of Winterton-on-Sea has a wonderful coastal landscape of undulating dunes and a wide expanse of sand. It is one of the most popular beaches in the area for families to have a bracing stroll by the sea.

This picture was taken on a blustery December morning as the first light of day hit the marram grasses.

BELOW A view northwards from the top of the dunes at Winterton-on-Sea, looking towards Horsey.

ABOVE A study of the dunes at Winterton-on-Sea as they sway in the wind and are turned golden by early morning light.

RIGHT Early morning light on the dunes at Winterton-on-Sea.

HORSEY

BELOW The expansive dunes remain a dominant feature of the coastal landscape as we reach Horsey, pictured here on a very dramatic late summer morning.

Horsey is more famous locally for its beautiful windmill a mile or so inland, but its beach and dunes, like those at Winterton-on-Sea, are a real gem.

This part of the coast between Winterton-on-Sea and Horsey is a great place to view seals and their pups, who are quite happy to bask on the shoreline, despite attracting large numbers of people intent on watching these lovely creatures.

RIGHT Wild conditions with the sand sculpted into distinctive shapes and plenty of white water at Horsey.

WAXHAM AND SEA PALLING

The tragic floods of 1953 left their mark on the coastline of Norfolk, and the fear of further breeching of sea defences has led to the construction of offshore reefs between Waxham and Sea Palling. This picture shows the beach at Waxham with a more traditional form of sea defence in the form of these well weathered groynes and large granite boulders.

Unfortunately, while the reefs have improved things at Sea Palling, they can lead to erosion taking place elsewhere in the local area.

ABOVE The last light of day touches the top of the dunes at Waxham on a calm midsummer evening.

RIGHT Intense early morning colours at Sea Palling, showing the posts that mark the positions of the offshore reefs.

The offshore reefs have certainly helped restore the beach to Sea Palling if the submerged steps are anything to go by.

HAPPISBURGH AND CART GAP

Cart Gap is a small coastal village just south of Happisburgh. Like its larger neighbour, it is a fascinating place to watch the North Sea on a stormy day.

This picture shows the lifeboat ramp, which has since been replaced by a more sturdier concrete structure.The ramp is used by the Happisburgh Lifeboat, who lost their own ramp to coastal erosion many years ago.

RIGHT ABOVE Happisburgh is an absolutely fascinating place. Blighted by years of intense coastal erosion from a North Sea that seems to have an added intensity here. Its sea defences from the 1950s (with a few modern additions of granite boulders) simply cannot cope with the power of the waves.

Properties on the cliff tops have succumbed to the sea as the crumbling cliffs are eaten away in very measurable terms year by year. The residents of the village have formed their own action group to seek government intervention. At present, however, nothing is happening to alleviate the problem.

This view from the ever-retreating cliffs south of the village shows the independently run Happisburgh Lighthouse, a distinctive and iconic symbol of this part of the Norfolk Coast.

RIGHT BELOW I would not have normally visited Happisburgh on a day as calm as this but I changed the plan for my original shoot once the sky started developing these wonderful pre-dawn colours. The old sea defences made great silhouettes against the fiery colours of the morning sky.

Early morning light on the beach and cliffs at Happisburgh. This picture was taken from one of the deposits of clay that can be found all over the beach to the south of the village. They form small 'islands', stubbornly standing up to the power of coastal erosion.

ABOVE Low tide on a stormy November day at Happisburgh.

RIGHT Since the destruction of the lifeboat slope, the metal steps are the main access to the beach at Happisburgh. On a stormy day with a high tide the steps will be literally shaken by the power of the waves and the wind.

It is clear from this picture that the old sea defences are nearing complete destruction. Gaps are constantly appearing along their length, making the North Sea's progress to the bottom of the erosion prone cliffs all the easier.

WALCOTT

North of Happisburgh lies the small village of Walcott, where the cliffs give way for a short while before continuing at Bacton.

The road adjacent to the sea wall is usually busy with parked cars with their owners gazing out to sea.

Like Happisburgh, it is one of those places where the North Sea can have a real stormy intensity, as shown in this picture taken on a July morning.

Plenty of foam in evidence here at Walcott on a blustery January afternoon showing the view towards Bacton, home to a huge North Sea gas plant.

MUNDESLEY

Mundesley is a small seaside resort in a beautiful setting on the edge of some of the tallest cliffs in Norfolk. This picture shows the beach at low tide on a pleasant spring morning.

ABOVE Sunrise at Mundesley showing the chalk deposits on the beach, visible at low tide.

RIGHT Early morning light on a late-October morning at Mundesley.

TRIMINGHAM

LEFT The village of Trimingham sits atop the highest cliffs in Norfolk and luckily most of the properties are a good distance away from the cliff edge. This is another area of intense coastal erosion. A walk along the cliff edge or on the beach at Trimingham will highlight the evidence of many landslips that are a regular occurrence.

This picture was taken on a sunny August evening from the cliff tops just north of the village.

RIGHT It is not always easy to get to the beach itself from the village, as the path down the cliffs is treacherous, especially in wet weather. To view these dramatic cliffs from below it is usually best to walk from nearby Mundesley or Overstrand at low tide.

This picture shows sunset on an August evening.

BELOW This area of the cliffs between Trimingham and Overstrand looks like it could be from another country. The evidence of erosion is plain to see.

OVERSTRAND

LEFT Dawn at Overstrand, a quiet village popular as a holiday destination for those wanting to get away from the the crowds of the more larger resorts in the area. This picture was taken on a moody spring morning on the sea wall looking back towards Trimingham, and shows the small assortment of boats and tractors from the small fishing fleet of the village.

ABOVE Subtle colours at dawn at Overstrand, with the remnants of sandcastles from the previous day boldly standing up to the power of the North Sea.

RIGHT A study of sea defences at Overstrand.

CROMER

BELOW A November morning on the beach just east of Cromer.

RIGHT The popular seaside town of Cromer has a delightful and picturesque seafront to stroll along as well as a beautiful church and museums dedicated to life at sea.

This picture shows part of the fishing fleet at Cromer and the lovely Victorian buildings to be found on the seafront.

LB'S
Lifeboat Cafe
Lifeboat Cafe
YH205 JOANNE ELIZABETH
YH 214
RORY JAMES

A late autumn morning at Cromer looking eastwards.

ABOVE The dominating feature of Cromer's seafront is its beautiful pier. Like many British seaside resort piers, Cromer Pier has had a vary varied history and has changed much over the years. On one occasion, it was literally sliced in half by a barge that had escaped its moorings on a very stormy winter night in 1993.

Today it is a major local concert venue with popular summer and winter shows. Above all, it is a great place for simply strolling and taking in the sea air.

RIGHT Ominous looking clouds gather over Cromer in this view taken from the pier on a summer evening.

The beautiful building on the right of the picture is the Hôtel de Paris and just behind its elegant façade is the tower of the church of St Peter and St Paul.

EAST RUNTON AND WEST RUNTON

BELOW East Runton is a small village west of Cromer that is a popular holiday destination with its clifftop caravan sites. Evidence of coastal erosion is evident here at the base of the cliffs.

On this November afternoon I walked down the slipway to the beach and was surprised to see at least twenty surfers braving the freezing conditions.

RIGHT West Runton is another small costal village sitting atop the cliffs just east of Sheringham.The village is famous for the discovery of the bones of a mammoth in the cliff face, exposed after a violent storm in the early 1990s.

West Runton is an ideal place to visit to appreciate the varied geology of the Norfolk Coast. The beach and cliff base are rich in fossils and the beach even has its own sea stack, shown in this picture taken on a sunny summer morning.

SHERINGHAM

BELOW LEFT Until the arrival of the railways in the late 1880s Sheringham was merely a small fishing village. Today it is a popular seaside village in a lovely location with a lovely shingle and sand beach.

The village sits in a shallow dip in the cliffs. To the east is Beeston Hill, locally known as the Beeston Bump, which provides a beautiful panorama over the area, while at the west end of the village the cliffs gain height again and the beach becomes predominantly shingle.

This picture, taken on a summer morning at high tide, shows the seafront at Sheringham with the early light illuminating some boldly coloured beach huts.

BELOW Dramatic early morning light at Sheringham.

The village is the main station of the North Norfolk Railway. Known as the Poppy Line, the preserved railway runs from Sheringham to the market town of Holt.

BOTTOM Two fishing boats on the slipway at Sheringham at dawn.

LEFT Intense golden light at the beginning of a summer day. This image illustrates part of the large sea wall while on the shingle a fisherman gets his boat ready to go out.

ABOVE A study of the sea defences at Sheringham.

WEYBOURNE

LEFT The stretch of cliffs between Sheringham and Weybourne mark the start of a more lower-lying coast. Just west of the area pictured here the cliffs diminish and the coastal landscape becomes dominated by shingle beaches and saltmarshes. This picture shows the view eastwards from the cliffs at Weybourne.

RIGHT ABOVE The shingle beach at Weybourne has quite a dramatic slope and the shingle seems to amplify the sound of crashing waves on a stormy day. It is very popular with beach fishermen and there is also a small fleet of fishing boats that go out from the beach here. This image shows a beautiful sky on a summer evening at Weybourne.

RIGHT BELOW A view from the beach at Weybourne looking eastwards – the cliffs have all but disappeared.

In this picture a huge raincloud moves in from the south, slowly blocking out the winter sunshine.

SALTHOUSE

Late evening light on the shingle bank at Salthouse.

The village of Salthouse is set in a beautiful location between the saltmarshes that back on to the shingle beach and a high ridge to the south of the village, on which sits the beautiful church of St Nicholas.

CLEY-NEXT-THE-SEA

LEFT Cley-next-the-Sea was once a thriving medieval port until its harbour silted up. Today the village can hardly be described as next to the sea but it is a delightful place to visit. There is a nature reserve at Cley Marshes, which is one of the most popular birdwatching areas on the Norfolk Coast. It is also home to St Margaret's Church, a beautifully ornate thirteenth-century building, and Cley Mill, which is one of the iconic symbols of North Norfolk. Nowadays it is rented out as holiday accommodation.

This image of the mill was taken on a cold winter morning at dawn among the reed beds which had recently been harvested.

BELOW The shingle beach at Cley-next-the-Sea on a late summer morning.

The shingle at Cley-next-the Sea marks the beginning of a 4-mile shingle spit that reaches Blakeney Point, famous for its seals. Organised boat trips run from Blakeney or Morston Quay to Blakeney Point to view the seals. This is a much less demanding way to visit than the 8-mile return walk along the shingle.

BLAKENEY

Like its neighbour Cley-next-the-Sea, Blakeney was once a thriving port until its harbour silted up. Between the shingle spit of Blakeney Point and the village itself there is a myriad of creeks, mud, marshes and channels, typical of the scenery to be found for the next few miles west along the Norfolk Coast.

It is an immensely popular destination, with visitors coming to the village to walk the coastal paths, watch the beautiful skies over the harbour or try their luck crabbing on the quay wall.

This picture shows one of the channels that flow to Blakeney Quay from Blakeney Harbour. The name of the boat is quite apt.

A view of the various craft to be found at Blakeney Quay with typical North Norfolk houses finished in flint in the distance.

OVERLEAF A very high tide at Blakeney is always a sight to behold. It is fascinating to see how quickly the tide comes in – its speed and power should never be underestimated.

Low tide on a moody spring morning at Blakeney Quay as a welcome sliver of light illuminates the boats in the foreground.

A phrase that is used regularly to describe Norfolk mentions its 'wide open skies'. This is never more fitting than on the North Norfolk Coast. In this example, the beautiful colours of a winter sunset are reflected in the mud at Blakeney.

MORSTON

LEFT Morston is the next village west from Blakeney. Being nearer to the entrance of Blakeney Harbour there are a lot more boats of all shapes and sizes to be found among the creeks and channels. At the height of summer the numbers of craft sailing at high tide have to be seen to be believed.

Morston Quay is one of the places where you can take a boat trip out to Blakeney point to view the seals.

This image to the east of the quay looking towards Blakeney shows a traditional Norfolk boat on a gorgeous spring evening.

RIGHT A calm summer evening at Morston Quay, with two very different boats in very different states of repair. On wandering around the creeks it is always fascinating to see the types of craft that are left abandoned to the elements.

RIGHT A beautiful winter morning sky at Morston Quay.

BELOW A previous high tide has left a fair amount of water on the edge of the quay at Morston on a winter day with beautiful colours in the sky.

Low tide on a winter morning at Morston Quay. The jetties in the picture are those used for the seal trips to Blakeney Point.

STIFFKEY

The village of Stiffkey is set in a beautiful location bordered inland by rolling countryside and seaward by a huge expanse of saltmarsh. The coast road passes through its very narrow but pretty main street.

This picture of the saltmarshes on a stormy July evening shows the pretty sea lavender that cover the saltmarshes for an all too brief period during the summer.

A general view of the small harbour at Stiffkey on a summer evening.

An expanse of mud and marsh as far as the eye can see. Stiffkey Marshes are a maze of twists and turns. These small footbridges help the traverse over this slippery environment.

If you choose to walk out into the marshes here it is imperative you know the tide times and are sure of your way back.

RIGHT A typical North Norfolk scene at Stiffkey harbour with a lone boat in a channel at low tide.

WELLS-NEXT-THE-SEA

Wells-next-the-Sea is a harbour town full of character. Once a thriving port, it is now a popular holiday destination and a favourite all-year-round day trip destination.

This picture shows the quay at low tide as a massive rainstorm passes over the town.

This picture, taken at twilight in winter, shows the quay at Wells-next-the-Sea with the pontoon moorings and granary building with its distinctive gantry in the background.

A stunning rainbow over the harbour at Wells-next-the-Sea.

To the left of the picture is the long sea wall that stretches a mile towards the beach. To the right of the picture are the Wells saltmarshes, the largest on the Norfolk Coast. At very high tides the saltmarshes are completely flooded, thus changing the look of the coastal landscape here dramatically.

Backed by lovely pinewoods that stretch as far as Holkham Bay, Wells-next-the-Sea Beach is quite rightly one of the most popular beaches on the Norfolk Coast.

Its beach huts, like those at so many seaside resorts in the UK, now command staggeringly high prices for those who want their little place by the sand and sea.

The beach huts are pictured on a November afternoon amid a layering of fresh snow.

A midsummer morning with early light on the beach huts at Wells-next-the-Sea.

HOLKHAM BAY

Holkham Bay is a simply stunning area of natural beauty and is justifiably one of the most popular walking destinations on the Norfolk Coast. The bay is part of the Holkham Nature Reserve which has a varied landscape of dunes, pine woodlands, saltmarshes and, above all, miles of golden sand within its boundaries

There is an overwhelming feeling of space here. I would challenge anyone not to be suitably moved by the bay's beauty.

This picture shows the bay on a stormy late summer morning looking westwards.

Late evening in summer with the last light of day bathing the marram grass and dunes in golden light.

This dramatic sunrise was taken at Holkham Gap, a semi-circular bay which can fill up completely at high tide. It is another place where simply watching a very high tide coming in is quite a spectacle as the sea fills up the bay covering over the hundreds of footprints in the mud and sand of those who have walked at Holkham on that day.

Fleeting light and an intensely grey-blue stormy sky make ideal photographic conditions in this picture taken on a stormy September morning.

In this picture the area of saltmarsh can be seen to the left and the extent of the pinewoods that back part of the bay can be clearly seen.

My favourite approach to Holkham Bay is via the footpath from Burnham Overy Staithe. The large dune system at the west end of the bay is simply beautiful. There are stunning views to be had here over the bay and back inland from on top of the dunes.

This picture shows a summer sunrise in hazy conditions.

A view eastwards from the top of the dunes at dawn, with mist hanging in between the wonderfully contoured landscape.

The first light of a winter morning on the dunes at the west end of the bay.

Low tide and the last light of a winter day at the west end of the bay. This picture was taken looking westwards towards the entrance to Burnham Harbour and Scolt Head Island.

BURNHAM OVERY STAITHE

Burnham Overy Staithe is a small coastal village with excellent facilities for sailing and boating enthusiasts. The village is connected to the sea via Burnham Harbour at the west end of Holkham Bay.

It is one of the North Norfolk Burnham villages, all named after the River Burn, around which they are grouped. The most famous Burnham villages are Burnham Thorpe, the birthplace of Lord Nelson, and Burnham Market, locally known as 'Chelsea on Sea'.

This picture shows a spring evening at Burnham Overy Staithe.

TOP Low tide on a spring evening looking back towards the village. To the left of the picture is the raised bank that forms the pathway to reach the west end of Holkham Bay. Very low tides present opportunities to visit areas of the marshes rarely explored if one can make it across the incredibly slippery mud. The beautiful and peaceful Scolt Head Island is a popular walk from Burnham Overy Staithe on a very low tide.

ABOVE Beautiful subtle hues in the sky pictured in this winter scene looking northwards at dawn, with the coastal path to the right of the picture.

OVERLEAF A typically beautiful North Norfolk sunset at Burnham Overy Staithe.

SCOLT HEAD ISLAND

Scolt Head Island is a barrier island which was created by the forces of nature binding sand, shingle and plant life to form this distinctive part of the Norfolk Coast. It is an area of peacefulness and wildness and is protected as a nature reserve.

Many visit the island on day boating trips from nearby Burnham Overy Staithe, while very low tides can make it accessible by foot.

This picture shows the marker buoy for the entrance to Burnham Harbour taken at a low tide when the water channel between the sands of Holkham Bay and Scolt Head Island was merely a few feet across and a few inches deep.

Dinghies lined up on the sands at Scolt Head Island on a summer evening looking back towards Burnham Overy Staithe. To the left of the picture is the Burnham Harbour channel.

Late evening light on the dunes at Scolt Head Island.

There are many places on the Norfolk Coast where you can feel as if you are the only person for miles around. That feeling is intensified when you visit Scolt Head Island.

BURNHAM DEEPDALE

ABOVE A short walk along the coastal path from Burnham Overy Staithe is the small village of Burnham Deepdale.

This summer picture shows the sea lavender in bloom with a lone boat sitting on the saltmarshes. The channel of water in the picture is Norton Creek, which divides the saltmarshes from Scolt Head Island in the distance.

RIGHT An abandoned boat among the creeks and saltmarshes on a moody summer evening at Burnham Deepdale, looking westwards towards Brancaster Staithe.

A summer evening's last light subtly illuminates a boat in a creek between Burnham Deepdale and Brancaster Staithe.

Abandoned boats on a spring evening among the saltmarshes
at Burnham Deepdale.

BRANCASTER STAITHE

A view of Malthouse Yard Quay at Brancaster Staithe. This lovely location has wonderful vistas across Brancaster Harbour, which will be, depending on your time of visit, a sea of mud or an expanse of water.

Brancaster Staithe is a popular spot for sailing and is home to its own sailing club.

For me, the most fascinating place is around Malthouse Yard Quay, which has been redeveloped to improve conditions for the small fishing fleet that sails from here. It is a chaotic scene with abandoned fishing equipment everywhere and every step you take makes a crunching sound as you stand on thousands of discarded seashells.

A moody-looking sky on a spring afternoon at Brancaster Staithe.

Low tide at Brancaster
Staithe on a stormy evening.

A view of the sailing dinghies stored at Brancaster Staithe, taken on a late summer evening.

BRANCASTER

Brancaster has a huge beach, which attracts walkers and families. At the western end of the beach on a windy day you will often find kites being flown, and kite surfing and even land yachting taking place.

This picture from the eastern end of the beach shows the entrance to Brancaster Harbour and beyond the channel of water is the western end of Scolt Head Island.

Just visible on the sands between the harbour and Scolt Head Island lies the wreck of the SS *Vina*. The temptation to cross the channel and visit the wreck is too much for some but the strength of the currents and speed of the tides are not to be trifled with.

A dramatic July sunset at low tide at Brancaster Beach.

Between the village and the beach is a large area of saltmarsh. The road that goes through the marshes connecting the village to the beach can become flooded at high tide, thus extending your stay at the beach if you are unaware of the tide times.

A view of the western end of Brancaster Beach on a winter afternoon.

TITCHWELL

Titchwell is famous for its RSPB reserve, which attracts thousands of birding enthusiasts every year.

Like Brancaster Beach, Titchwell Beach is a large expanse of sand which at low tide reveals its former use as a firing range during the Second World War, with the remains of an old gunnery tower clearly visible as you approach the beach along the path from the nature reserve. There are even a couple of tanks buried in the sand, which are visible occasionally.

This picture of a dramatic sunset was taken at the western end of Titchwell Beach.

LEFT There are always plenty of shells to be found on the beach at Titchwell as can be seen in this picture taken on a late spring evening.

BELOW A study of shells on Titchwell Beach.

THORNHAM

Thornham is a very pretty village with a small harbour, whose entrance is between the beaches of Titchwell and Holme.

Today just a handful of boats moor in the harbour, which was once a larger port.

This picture shows the saltmarshes and creeks around the harbour on a moody November afternoon.

These posts at Thornham are so photogenic. They were probably used as protection for the harbour wall when the village had a thriving port.

Here they are illuminated by the low winter sun. The raised area to the right of the picture was once the site of a granary.

Thornham is another place in North Norfolk where it is quite a spectacle to watch a very high tide come in.

This picture, taken on a beautiful summer evening, shows the view towards Holme Dunes in the distance to the left.

Approximately half an hour separates this picture from the previous one. The high tide is now fully in and will start going back out almost straight away, while I have to sit it out until I am safe to drive off the raised car park, which is literally a few feet behind where my camera was set up.

HOLME DUNES

The beautiful dunes at Holme Dunes Nature Reserve can be reached via the coastal path from Thornham or from the village of Holme-next-the-Sea. The reserve is a haven for birdwatching and is one of the most peaceful areas of this part of the coast.

It is at this point that the waters of the North Sea meet with the waters of the Wash and the coast starts to face westwards.

This picture shows the beautiful dunes on a spring evening.

HUNSTANTON

Hunstanton, or 'Sunny Hunny' as it is affectionately known, is a lovely seaside resort on the west coast of Norfolk with some of the most distinctive cliffs in the United Kingdom, formed of red and white chalk and carstone.

Hunstanton is divided into two parts – the village of Old Hunstanton and the newer town of Hunstanton St Edmund, which is home to most of the seaside-based attractions.

This picture shows the view from the beach at Old Hunstanton with Hunstanton Lighthouse visible on the clifftop.

The west-facing aspect of Hunstanton means that sunsets are often spectacular affairs.

In this picture, taken at sunset on a moody spring evening, the low tide has exposed these wonderfully rounded seaweed covered boulders.

Beautiful light on the cliffs at Old Hunstanton as the tide starts to come in on a summer evening.

Sunset at Old Hunstanton, showing an old wreck trapped in the sand.

HEACHAM AND SNETTISHAM

It is possible to walk along a sea wall between Hunstanton and Snettisham passing through the seaside village of Heacham on the way with lovely views across the Wash.

The Wash is a roughly square-shaped estuary and is a wonderful place to view sunsets with the colours reflected in the sea or in the huge expanse of mud visible at low tide.

This picture was taken from the dunes at Heacham at sunset in mid-summer.

ABOVE Distinctive cloud formations in this picture taken between Heacham and Snettisham.

In this instance the tide is low and the vastness of the mudflats is clearly visible.

RIGHT Low tide at Snettisham on a humid summer afternoon.

Directly across the Wash the county of Lincolnshire is 15 miles away. It is here that my photographic journey around the beautiful and varied Norfolk Coast comes to an end.

INDEX